JUL 0 3 2017

I LOVE MUSIC

Pop

Aaron Carr

www.av2books.com

LET'S READ

AV²
BY WEIGL™
ADDED VALUE • AUDIO VISUAL

Go to **www.av2books.com**, and enter this book's unique code.

BOOK CODE

G 8 6 5 6 6 9

AV² by Weigl brings you media enhanced books that support active learning.

AV² provides enriched content that supplements and complements this book. Weigl's AV² books strive to create inspired learning and engage young minds in a total learning experience.

Your AV² Media Enhanced books come alive with...

Audio
Listen to sections of the book read aloud.

Video
Watch informative video clips.

Embedded Weblinks
Gain additional information for research.

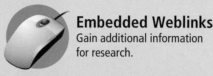

Try This!
Complete activities and hands-on experiments.

Key Words
Study vocabulary, and complete a matching word activity.

Quizzes
Test your knowledge.

Slide Show
View images and captions, and prepare a presentation.

... and much, much more!

Published by AV² by Weigl
350 5th Avenue, 59th Floor
New York, NY 10118
Website: www.av2books.com

Library of Congress Cataloging-in-Publication Data

Carr, Aaron.
 Pop / Aaron Carr.
    pages cm. -- (I love music)
 Includes bibliographical references and index.
 ISBN 978-1-4896-3585-3 (hard cover : alk. paper) -- ISBN 978-1-4896-3586-0 (soft cover : alk. paper)
 ISBN 978-1-4896-3587-7 (single user ebook) -- ISBN 978-1-4896-3588-4 (multi-user ebook)
 1. Popular music--History and criticism--Juvenile literature. I. Title.
 ML3470.C37 2015
 781.6309--dc23
                              2015003070

Printed in the United States of America in Brainerd, Minnesota
1 2 3 4 5 6 7 8 9 0   19 18 17 16 15

062015
170415

Project Coordinator: Jared Siemens
Designer: Mandy Christiansen

The publisher acknowledges Getty Images and iStock as the primary image suppliers for this title.

Pop

CONTENTS

2   AV² Book Code
4   When did Pop Start?
6   Where did Pop Come From?
8   Early Pop Songs
10   Singing Pop
12   What Are Pop Songs About?
14   Instruments
16   In a Band
18   Pop Today
20   I Love Music
22   Pop Facts
24   Key Words/Log on to www.av2books.com

I love music. Pop is my favorite kind of music.

Pop music started in the United States during the 1950s.

Pop comes from many different kinds of music.

The first pop music came from rock songs.

The first pop songs were easy to learn. People listened to them on the radio.

Pop songs are made to be enjoyed by everyone.

Pop singers may sing very loud or very soft. They have to practice to hit high and low notes.

Listening to pop
may make you
want to dance.

Pop songs are often about love and happy memories.

Some pop songs are about feeling sad.

Pop songs are played on many different instruments. Drums and guitars are often used in pop.

Today's pop music is sometimes made on computers.

I like to play pop
with my friends.
Each person plays
a different instrument.

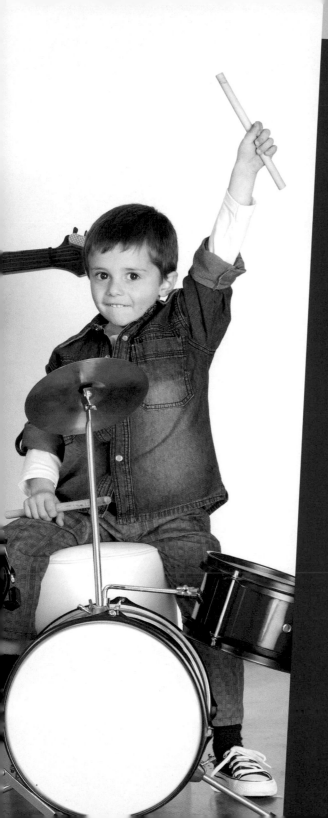

I learn how to be part of a team by playing in a band.

Many pop concerts have dancers and costumes.

One Direction held the most popular concerts of 2014.

I love pop music. Playing music helps me learn new things.

POP FACTS

These pages provide detailed information that expands on the interesting facts found in the book. They are intended to be used by adults as a learning support to help young readers round out their knowledge of each musical genre featured in the *I Love Music* series.

Pages 4–5

I love music. Pop is my favorite kind of music. Music is the name given to sounds made with voices or musical instruments and put together in a way that conveys emotion. People use music to express themselves. Pop started as a shortening of "popular music," which refers to whatever music is well-liked in a specific period of time. As such, the genre is constantly changing with current music trends.

Pages 6–7

Pop comes from many different kinds of music. Pop music came about as a result of large groups of people liking the same songs. Some of the first pop songs, by modern definition, were rock and roll songs. In the mid-1950s, rock songs began to replace jazz and folk songs at the top of the charts. Bill Haley's "Rock Around the Clock" was one of the first rock and roll songs to top popular music charts.

Pages 8–9

The first pop songs were easy to learn. Pop songs are often short, simple, and catchy, with memorable hooks, because they are designed to appeal to the widest audience possible. Radio stations in the 1950s started playing more music for teenagers in an attempt to take advantage of young people's spending power. Radio was, and still is, important in determining trends in pop music.

Pages 10–11

Pop singers may sing very loud or very soft. Pop singers are among the most versatile vocalists in music. A pop singer may switch from speech-quality vocals to belting, a type of loud and forceful singing. An exercise called "sirening" has been known to help pop singers increase their vocal range. They sing an "ng" sound from the top to the bottom of their range and back again, like a police siren.

**Pages
12–13**

Pop songs are often about love and happy memories. Early pop music's radio-friendly sensibility led to a large library of upbeat songs with lyrics focused on love, hope, and nostalgia. However, sad pop songs are also common. A 2014 study of pop lyrics from the 1960s to the 2000s showed that common pop themes include pain, loss, and rebellion.

**Pages
14–15**

Pop songs are played with many different instruments. Pop music uses a wide variety of different instruments, though pianos, keyboards, electric guitars, basses, and drums are most common. Today, computer-generated instruments and beats are often used to craft pop songs. Programs such as Auto-Tune help singers to stay in key. Much like rock music, a variety of other instruments may be used in pop songs, such as the saxophone or violin.

**Pages
16–17**

I like to play pop with my friends. Playing music with others helps teach children cooperation, teamwork, and how to achieve goals. Children who regularly play music tend to have more confidence and get along better with others. Some students learn better in groups because they do not feel the pressure of having to learn on their own.

**Pages
18–19**

Many pop concerts have dancers and costumes. Pop concerts have grown from simple live performances to large-scale theatrical spectacles. Past and present pop artists, such as Michael Jackson, Madonna, Katy Perry, and Lady Gaga, employ teams of dancers for their live shows. Pop concerts may also include sophisticated lighting effects, pyrotechnics, multimedia screens, and elaborate costumes. More than 3.4 million people attended One Direction concerts during the pop group's worldwide tour in 2014.

**Pages
20–21**

I love pop music. Playing music helps me learn new things. Recent studies suggest that learning and practicing music can be beneficial to a child's ability to learn. Among these benefits are improved motor skills and dexterity, increased test scores, and even raised Intelligence Quotient, or IQ, scores. Learning music at an early age has also been shown to aid in language development, and to improve reading and listening skills.

KEY WORDS

Research has shown that as much as 65 percent of all written material published in English is made up of 300 words. These 300 words cannot be taught using pictures or learned by sounding them out. They must be recognized by sight. This book contains 52 common sight words to help young readers improve their reading fluency and comprehension. This book also teaches young readers several important content words. These words are paired with pictures to aid in learning and improve understanding.

Page	Sight Words First Appearance
4	I, is, kind, my, of
5	in, states, the
6	comes, different, from, many
7	came, first, songs
8	learn, on, people, them, to, were
9	are, be, by, made
10	and, have, high, may, or, they, very
11	make, want, you
12	about, often
13	some
15	sometimes
16	a, each, like, play, with
17	how, part
19	most, one
21	helps, me, new, things

Page	Content Words First Appearance
4	music, pop
5	United States
8	radio
10	notes, singers
11	dance
12	memories
14	drums, guitars, instruments
15	computers
17	band, team
18	concerts, costumes, dancers
19	One Direction

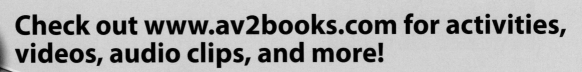

Check out www.av2books.com for activities, videos, audio clips, and more!

1 Go to www.av2books.com.

2 Enter book code. G 8 6 5 6 6 9

3 Fuel your imagination online!

www.av2books.com